BIG PICTURE 📷 SPORTS

Meet the
LOS ANGELES
RAMS

BY
ZACK BURGESS

NORWOOD HOUSE 🏠 PRESS

CHICAGO, ILLINOIS

NORWOOD HOUSE PRESS

P.O. Box 316598 • Chicago, Illinois 60631
For more information about Norwood House Press please visit our website at
www.norwoodhousepress.com or call 866-565-2900.

Photo Credits:
All photos courtesy of Associated Press, except for the following: Black Book Archives (6, 7, 15, 18),
Bowman Gum Co. (10 both), Topps, Inc. (11 top & middle, 22, 23), Sports Illustrated for Kids (11 bottom).

Cover Photo: Jeff Roberson/Associated Press

The football memorabilia photographed for this book is part of the authors' collection. The collectibles used
for artistic background purposes in this series were manufactured by many different card companies—
including Bowman, Donruss, Fleer, Leaf, O-Pee-Chee, Pacific, Panini America, Philadelphia Chewing Gum,
Pinnacle, Pro Line, Pro Set, Score, Topps, and Upper Deck—as well as several food brands, including
Crane's, Hostess, Kellogg's, McDonald's and Post.

Designer: Ron Jaffe
Series Editors: Mike Kennedy and Mark Stewart
Project Management: Black Book Partners, LLC.
Editorial Production: Lisa Walsh

LIBRARY OF CONGRESS CATALOGING-IN-PUBLICATION DATA
Names: Burgess, Zack.
Title: Meet the Los Angeles Rams / by Zack Burgess.
Description: Chicago, Illinois : Norwood House Press, 2016. | Series: Big
    picture sports | Includes bibliographical references and index.
Identifiers: LCCN 2015026010| ISBN 9781599537443 (library edition : alk.
    paper) | ISBN 9781603578479 (ebook)
Subjects: LCSH: Los Angeles Rams (Football team : 2016-)--Juvenile
    literature. | St. Louis Rams (Football team)--History--Juvenile literature.
Classification: LCC GV956.S85 B87 2016 | DDC 796.332/640977866--dc23 LC record
    available at https://lccn.loc.gov/2015026010

288N—072016
Manufactured in the United States of America in North Mankato, Minnesota

CONTENTS

Words in **bold type** are defined on page 24.

The Rams play with amazing joy and energy.

4

CALL ME A RAM

The Los Angeles Rams are
named after an animal that loves
to "butt heads" with opponents.
That makes sense. The Rams are
known for their speed, and hard
blocking and tackling. They love
to play old-time football. But they
are also willing to try new ideas.

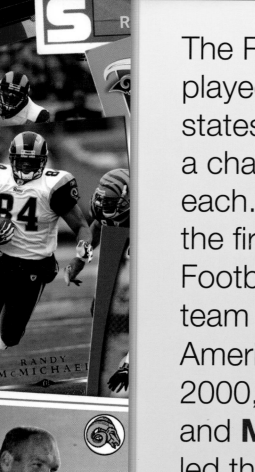

The Rams have played in three states. They won a championship in each. They also were the first National Football League (NFL) team to sign African American players. In 2000, Kurt Warner and **Marshall Faulk** led them to their first Super Bowl victory.

Kurt Warner was one of the best passers in team history.

In California, the Rams have always played outdoors.

Best Seat in the House

Over the years, the Rams have played home games indoors and outdoors. From 1995 to 2015, they played in a domed stadium in St. Louis, Missouri. Before that, they hosted games in outdoor stadiums in Cleveland, Ohio and Los Angeles, California.

SHOE BOX

The trading cards on these pages show some of the best Rams ever.

ELROY HIRSCH

RECEIVER · 1949–1957

Elroy was nicknamed "Crazy Legs" because of the odd way he ran. He was an **All-Pro** twice.

NORM VAN BROCKLIN

QUARTERBACK · 1949–1957

Norm could throw the ball a long way. His 73-yard touchdown pass won the 1951 NFL championship.

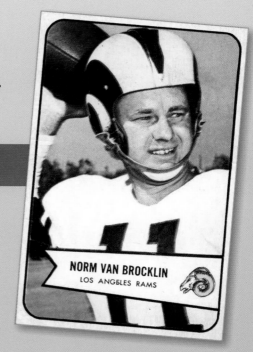

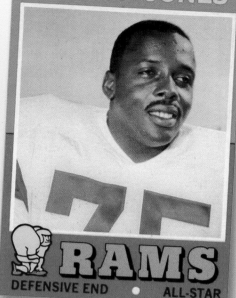

DEACON JONES

DEFENSIVE END · 1961-1971

No one was better at chasing down quarterbacks than Deacon. In fact, he invented the term "**sack**!"

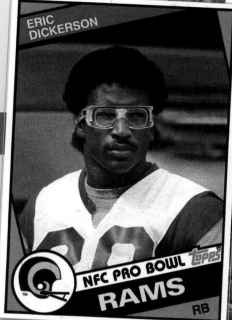

ERIC DICKERSON

RUNNING BACK · 1983-1987

Eric was a fast and powerful runner. He set an NFL record with 2,105 rushing yards in 1984.

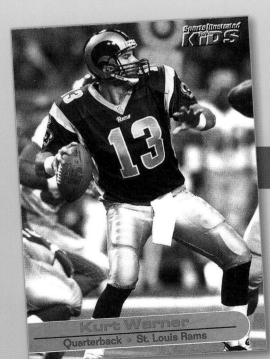

KURT WARNER

QUARTERBACK · 1998-2003

Kurt had a strong, accurate arm. He was voted the NFL's Most Valuable Player (MVP) twice with the Rams.

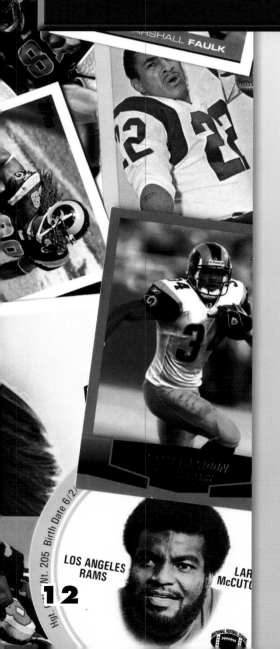

THE BIG PICTURE

Look at the two photos on page 13. Both appear to be the same. But they are not. There are three differences. Can you spot them?

Answers on page 23.

TRUE OR FALSE?

Marshall Faulk was a star running back. Two of these facts about him are **TRUE**. One is **FALSE**. Do you know which is which?

1. Marshall was drafted to play Major League Baseball.

2. Marshall liked to butt heads with teammates before games, just like a ram.

3. Marshall had more than 1,000 yards rushing and receiving in 1999.

Answer on page 23.

Marshall Faulk bursts into the end zone.

Fans in Los Angeles celebrate the return of the Rams.

Go Rams, Go!

The Rams have fans all over the country. They have always been loud and proud. When the Rams returned to California in 2016, many people there cried tears of joy. For them, it was a dream come true.

ON THE MAP

Here is a look at where five Rams were born, along with a fun fact about each.

 MERLIN OLSEN • LOGAN, UTAH
Merlin played in the **Pro Bowl** 14 times.

 JACKIE SLATER • JACKSON, MISSISSIPPI
Jackie was voted into the **Hall of Fame** in 2001.

 BOB WATERFIELD • ELMIRA, NEW YORK
Bob was the NFL's MVP when the Rams played in Cleveland.

 JACK YOUNGBLOOD • JACKSONVILLE, FLORIDA
Jack played in the Super Bowl with a broken leg.

 TOM FEARS • GUADALAJARA, MEXICO
Tom once caught 18 passes in a game for the Rams.

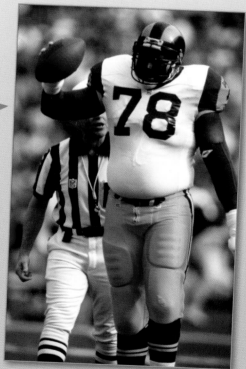

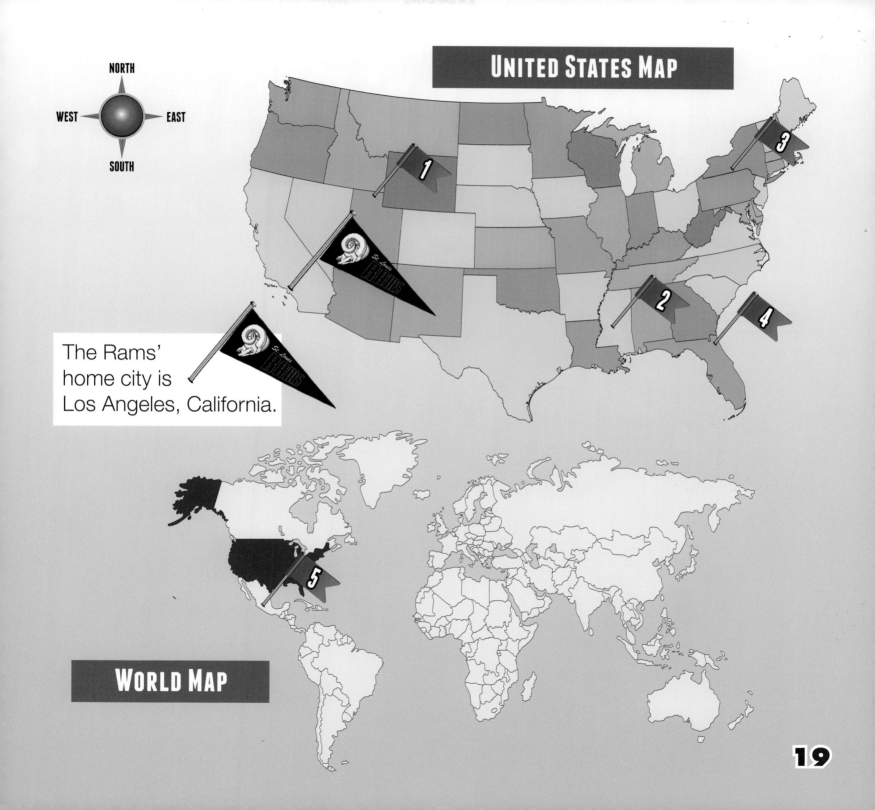

UNITED STATES MAP

The Rams' home city is Los Angeles, California.

WORLD MAP

19

HOME AND AWAY

Todd Gurley wears the Rams' home uniform.

Football teams wear different uniforms for home and away games. The main colors of the Rams are blue, white, and gold. For many years, they used a gold that was closer to yellow.

Aaron Donald wears the Rams' away uniform.

The Rams' helmet has a ram's horn on each side. The Rams were the first team to put a design on their helmet. They began using the horns in 1948.

WE WON!

ISAAC **BRUCE**

WIDE RECEIVER

The Rams won their first NFL title in 1945, when the team played in Cleveland. They won their second in Los Angeles, in 1951. They won their first Super Bowl after the 1999 season, as the St. Louis Rams. **Isaac Bruce** caught the game-winning touchdown pass.

RECORD BOOK

These Rams set team records.

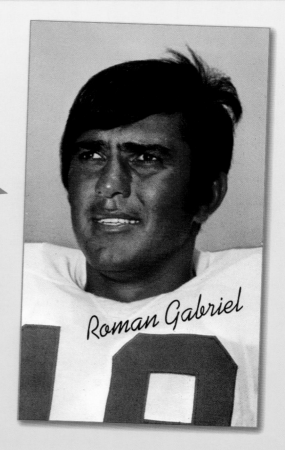

Roman Gabriel

TOUCHDOWN PASSES	RECORD
Season: Kurt Warner (1999)	41
Career: **Roman Gabriel**	154

TOUCHDOWN CATCHES	RECORD
Season: Elroy Hirsch (1951)	17
Career: Isaac Bruce	84

RUSHING YARDS	RECORD
Season: Eric Dickerson (1984)	2,105
Career: Steven Jackson	10,138

ANSWERS FOR THE BIG PICTURE
The stripe on the pants of the player on the far left changed color, #14 changed to #18, and #26 disappeared.

ANSWER FOR TRUE AND FALSE
#2 is false. Marshall did not butt heads with teammates.

Football Words

All-Pro
An honor given to the best NFL player at each position.

Hall of Fame
The museum in Canton, Ohio, where football's greatest players are honored.

Pro Bowl
The NFL's annual all-star game.

Sack
A tackle of the quarterback that loses yardage.

Index

Photos are on **BOLD** numbered pages.

About the Author

Zack Burgess has been writing about sports for more than 20 years. He has lived all over the country and interviewed lots of All-Pro football players, including Brett Favre, Eddie George, Jerome Bettis, Shannon Sharpe, and Rich Gannon. Zack was the first African American beat writer to cover Major League Baseball when he worked for the *Kansas City Star*.

About the Rams

Learn more at these websites:

www.therams.com • www.profootballhof.com

www.teamspiritextras.com/Overtime/html/rams.html